IF FOUND PL

👤 _____

✉ _____

📱 _____

Greater Than a Tourist Book Series
Reviews from Readers

I think the series is wonderful and beneficial for tourists to get information before visiting the city.

-Seckin Zumbul, Izmir Turkey

I am a world traveler who has read many trip guides but this one really made a difference for me. I would call it a heartfelt creation of a local guide expert instead of just a guide.

-Susy, Isla Holbox, Mexico

New to the area like me, this is a must have!

 -Joe, Bloomington, USA

This is a good series that gets down to it when looking for things to do at your destination without having to read a novel for just a few ideas.

-Rachel, Monterey, USA

Good information to have to plan my trip to this destination.

-Pennie Farrell, Mexico

Great ideas for a port day.

-Mary Martin USA

Aptly titled, you won't just be a tourist after reading this book. You'll be greater than a tourist!

-Alan Warner, Grand Rapids, USA

Even though I only have three days to spend in San Miguel in an upcoming visit, I will use the author's suggestions to guide some of my time there. An easy read - with chapters named to guide me in directions I want to go.

-Robert Catapano, USA

Great insights from a local perspective! Useful information and a very good value!

-Sarah, USA

This series provides an in-depth experience through the eyes of a local. Reading these series will help you to travel the city in with confidence and it'll make your journey a unique one.

-Andrew Teoh, Ipoh, Malaysia

GREATER THAN A TOURIST- NEW JERSEY USA

50 Travel Tips from a Local

Andrew Seitz

Cover designed by: Ivana Stamenkovic
Cover Image: https://pixabay.com/en/cape-may-new-jersey-houses-street-
105590/

CZYK Publishing Since 2011.

Greater Than a Tourist
Visit our website at www.GreaterThanaTourist.com

Lock Haven, PA
All rights reserved.
ISBN: 9781724108906

>TOURIST

50 TRAVEL TIPS FROM A LOCAL

BOOK DESCRIPTION

Are you excited about planning your next trip?

Do you want to try something new?

Would you like some guidance from a local?

If you answered yes to any of these questions, then this Greater Than a Tourist book is for you.

Greater Than a Tourist New Jersey by Andrew Seitz offers the inside scoop on New Jersey. Most travel books tell you how to travel like a tourist. Although there is nothing wrong with that, as part of the Greater Than a Tourist series, this book will give you travel tips from someone who has lived at your next travel destination.

In these pages, you will discover advice that will help you throughout your stay. This book will not tell you exact addresses or store hours but instead will give you excitement and knowledge from a local that you may not find in other smaller print travel books.

Travel like a local. Slow down, stay in one place, and get to know the people and the culture. By the time you finish this book, you will be eager and prepared to travel to your next destination.

TABLE OF CONTENTS

13. FOOD: TRY TO FIND A FARMERS MARKET OR ROADSIDE VEGETABLE STAND

14. FOOD: ON SANDWICHES (AND BURGERS)

15. FOOD: PORK ROLL IS FANTASTIC

16. FOOD: DINERS

17. FOOD: ALMOST ANY PIZZA IS GOOD

18. FOOD: INDIAN FOOD

19. FOOD: WEGMAN'S IS BETTER THAN WHOLE FOODS

20. FOOD: MICROBREWERIES

21. FOOD: BE CAUTIOUS WITH SEAFOOD

22. ATTRACTIONS: THEATERS

23. ATTRACTIONS: HIKING AND BIKING

24. ATTRACTIONS: WATER ACTIVITIES

25. ATTRACTIONS: SPORTING EVENTS

26. ATTRACTIONS: GROUNDS FOR SCULPTURE

27. ATTRACTIONS: FISHING AND HUNTING

28. ATTRACTIONS: MUSEUMS AND AQUARIUM

29. ATTRACTIONS: AMUSEMENT PARKS

30. ATTRACTIONS: SHOPPING

31. LOCATIONS: PRINCETON

32. LOCATIONS: ATLANTIC CITY

33. LOCATIONS: SMALL TOWNS

34. LOCATIONS: COASTAL TOWNS

Travel Bucket List

NOTES

DEDICATION

I dedicate this book to my parents for schlepping me all over God's green Earth as a child.

Also to CHC for helping me out to start and for inspiring me to leave New Jersey in the first place.

ABOUT THE AUTHOR

Andrew Seitz is a writer, digital marketer and SEO consultant who lives in Chicago. Seitz has been traveling since childhood, follows cars closely and dies a little each week thanks to the ineptitude of the Oakland Raiders.

Seitz was born and raised in New Jersey but moved to Chicago in 2018.

HOW TO USE THIS BOOK

The Greater Than a Tourist book series was written by someone who has lived in an area for over three months. The goal of this book is to help travelers either dream or experience different locations by providing opinions from a local. The author has made suggestions based on their own experiences. Please do your own research before traveling to the area in case the suggested places are unavailable.

FROM THE PUBLISHER

Traveling can be one of the most important parts of a person's life. The anticipation and memories that you have are some of the best. As a publisher of the Greater Than a Tourist book series, as well as the popular 50 Things to Know book series, we strive to help you learn about new places, spark your imagination, and inspire you. Wherever you are and whatever you do I wish you safe, fun, and inspiring travel.

Lisa Rusczyk Ed. D.
CZYK Publishing

OUR STORY

Traveling is a passion of the "Greater than a Tourist" series creator. Lisa studied abroad in college, and for their honeymoon Lisa and her husband toured Europe. During her travels to Malta, an older man tried to give her some advice based on his own experience living on the island since he was a young boy. She was not sure if she should talk to the stranger but was interested in his advice. When traveling to some places she was wary to talk to locals because she was afraid that they weren't being genuine. Through her travels, Lisa learned how much locals had to share with tourists. Lisa created the "Greater Than a Tourist" book series to help connect people with locals. A topic that locals are very passionate about sharing.

WELCOME TO
> TOURIST

INTRODUCTION

"Travel is fatal to prejudice,
bigotry and narrow-mindedness,
and many of our people need it
sorely on these accounts. Broad,
wholesome, charitable views of men
and things cannot be acquired by
vegetating in one little corner of the
earth all one's lifetime."

— Mark Twain, The Innocents Abroad

I grew up right outside of Princeton, as idyllic, upscale and well-heeled an area as you will find in the United States. My parents travelled extensively when I was younger and I, a mere child, accompanied them.

People would ask my parents where they were from and, after hearing New Jersey, they would either have a strained look or ask what exit they were off of. (Ha ha) As a child, it was always strange to me to hear people making fun of New Jersey, especially since the more I saw of the country, the more I realized just how nice Central New Jersey is.

I have travelled all over the United States and I have been to numerous other countries. I truly believe New Jersey is a fantastic state because of all of the variety it offers. From beaches to mountains and all points in between, you can find something to do and somewhere to go. The food scene is excellent, competitive and highly diverse. New Jersey has the best pizza in America and, by extension, likely the world.

When I picked up this assignment, I found the hardest thing was picking which topics not to cover. I avoided obvious advice, such as 'pack sunscreen' or 'it's hot in the summer and cold in the winter.'

Of course it's hot in the summer and cold in the winter.

To make reading this a tad easier, I have broken this up into five sections: Travel, Food, Locations, Attractions and Culture, for ease of use.

1. YOU HAVE PLENTY OF AIRPORT OPTIONS

Flying into New Jersey is great because there are so many options. It can also be a massive headache because there are so many options. Newark, JFK, Philadelphia and the lesser known Trenton-Mercer are your best options for easy travel. Determining which airport will be best for your trip depends on where you are staying. Trenton-Mercer only has smaller and budget airlines which have lower fares, but the airport has limited public transportation options. Prices are likely higher at Newark, JFK or Philadelphia, but you can take public transportation from those airports to almost anywhere on the east coast. Trenton-Mercer is a solid option if you are staying near the airport or packing light, as the budget airlines which fly there do not offer free checked baggage. If you are flying internationally, I would recommend Newark. I have flown both domestic and international, and Newark's customs section is as efficient as any airport in America. If you are looking for amenities such as lounges, look for flights to Philadelphia or JFK.

2. BE ON THE LOOKOUT FOR JUG HANDLES

I am comfortable with jug handle turns, but I was born and raised in New Jersey. I have travelled all over America, Canada and Europe, but I have only seen a handful of jug handle turns outside of New Jersey; hence the nickname, "Jersey Left." I know many people who visit New Jersey are confused by jug handles, so it deserves a mention. Jug handle turns are turns like highway entry or exit ramps, only on four lane roads. There are three types of jug handle turns: a standard forward jug handle; a standard reverse jug handle and a 90° jug handle which leads to a U-Turn. If you have a modern GPS system, you should be fine. If you do not have a GPS system, or your GPS system is malfunctioning, be on the lookout for roads which do not allow left turns. The right lane is where your turn will be. Occasionally, you exit the jug handle before your turn, occasionally after; you need to pay close attention to the specific jug handle you are coming up to.

3. TIPS ON THE TURNPIKE / PARKWAY

Odds are, if you end up renting a car or driving into New Jersey, you will end up on either the New Jersey Turnpike or New Jersey Parkway. Both roads are large capacity interstates which are wholly owned and operated by the state of New Jersey. If you are a AAA, AARP or Allstate Roadside member, you cannot get assistance from those organizations. You will need to contact the state operated roadside assistance program, instead. Most roadside assistance programs are well aware of this and will transfer your call to whatever company can help you if you try to contact them. You should also know about the EZ-Pass. The most efficient way to get through toll roads is by using EZ-Pass, a toll payment system usable in states up and down the coast and across the Midwest into Illinois. If you are renting a car and plan on traveling around the state or taking a day-trip, EZ-Pass is well worth the extra cost.

4. DRIVING ON THE HIGHWAYS

You know about roadside assistance and EZ-Pass, but let's talk about a few rules for driving on the highway; "don't be that person" tips. On the busiest highways, such as the aforementioned Turnpike and Parkway, as well as 287, 95, etc., speed-limits may appear arbitrary. I have found myself getting passed, blown past, even, going twenty to thirty miles an hour over the speed limit. An old joke about Pennsylvania drivers: they have nowhere to go and they are in no rush to get there. You will find there are a number of drivers in New Jersey who have places to go and they are rushing to get there. Do not go the speed limit in the left lane! If you are going the speed limit in the left lane, expect to be tailgated, expect to get honked at or expect to be flashed with high-beams. Also be aware of unsafe behavior. You may see people passing on the right side or attempting other dangerous moves. If you are familiar with similar 'city-driving' behavior you are not in for any surprises. I would advise you to exercise caution when passing or being passed. It's not "Death Race" out there or anything, but the drivers of NJ do tend to be more aggressive than most.

5. EVERY CIRCLE IS DIFFERENT; ADHERE TO YIELD SIGNS!

I am familiar with circles because I have family in Massachusetts and they live near circles. Studies show traffic circles as better at traffic management than most intersection types, so they will become more common as time goes on; get used to them. You must consider each individual traffic circle as you come to it. Massachusetts has many circles but the state has clearly defined rules on how to enter and exit them. People inside the circle have the right of way, and people on the inside lane of the circle have the right of way compared to people on the outside lane. I have always found those rules to be counterintuitive! New Jersey does not have unified circle rules. Every circle is different. I can personally recollect two separate circles in Mercer County having different rules. Unlike Massachusetts, the outside lane has the right of way. The circle rules differ on whether the car entering the circle has the right of way or whether the car inside the circle has the right of way. Look for yield signs as you approach the circle and obey them! Police tend to patrol those areas to pull over drivers who do not follow the signs.

6. POLICE AND DRIVING

While I mentioned the absurd speeds of the highways, driving on normal roads is different. Under normal circumstances, you will not get a ticket if you are going near the speed limit, up to 5mph over the limit. 5-10mph increases your chances of getting pulled over. If you're going 10mph+ over the speed limit and you see a police car, you should start locating your license, registration and insurance card. When it comes to the police in New Jersey, there are two sets: local and state police. I find state police to be far more professional. The State Police also write far more tickets and let far fewer drivers off with a warning. Do not accept tickets for violations you did not commit. There are a number of citations you can receive in New Jersey which are expensive and cannot be fought in court. "Failure to observe a traffic stop" or similar citation is more expensive than most moving violations and cannot be argued in court. The only exception is speeding: if offered a ticket which does not put points on your license, accept such a ticket without hesitation.

7. AVOID RT 1 IF YOU CAN

US Route One is a messy hodgepodge of highways, many of them among the oldest in America. Historically significant roads such as the Boston-Post Road from Boston to New York, the Baltimore Pike or the Lincoln Highway have all merged into one route. US Route One goes all the way up the East Coast, from the tip of Florida to a connecting road into Canada. If you find yourself on Route 1 during rush hour, even a short-trip might feel as long as a trip from Florida to Canada. Route 1 is centrally located and you will be guided to it by a number of GPS systems. Whenever and however possible, avoid Rt 1 like the plague. The road is congested and riddled with potholes. Frustrations can boil over in the rush hour traffic, which can slow to a crawl. In many cases the Route 1 is a 50mph zone while parallel roads are 45mph zones, less congested and better maintained. If you are visiting an area, business or location on Route 1, aim to find an alternative route which limits your time on Route 1.

8. BE CAREFUL AT INTERSECTIONS

Outside of major cities, I have found the drivers of New Jersey, Connecticut and Massachusetts to be the most aggressive in America. A common occurrence is the "Pittsburgh Left" — drivers gunning the throttle as soon as the light turns green to make a left turn. It can feel like a game, as both drivers try to get off the line first. Who will win, the driver making the left turn or the car across from them, trying to block their efforts? The answer is nobody wins and it's a stupid game. These situations can be testy and I've seen my share of nervous moments as a result. As a pedestrian, keep an eye out for cars racing across the road; you have the right of way but a car has both momentum and a substantial weight advantage. Cars will win that fight. I have seen near collisions because drivers are too busy getting across the road and they nearly hit pedestrians. As a driver, pay attention if you see a left turn-signal from the car across the intersection. There is no need to speed off the line, especially when it might cause an accident.

9. TRAVEL: PUBLIC TRANSPORTATION IS VIABLE

Due to its unique population density, New Jersey has a strong public transportation system. In many ways, New Jersey's transportation is as well coordinated as many major cities across America. Do you need to get from Hoboken to Rahway? There is a bus line and a train line which can help you. Even smaller towns tend to have public transportation options. Usually, this comes in the form of one or two bus lines which can take a passenger from a small town to a larger one. At larger towns or public destinations, such as a shopping mall, you could take any of a number of buses to get wherever you need to go. Between the trains, bus options and ride-sharing apps such as Uber and Lyft, you could probably survive a visit to New Jersey without needing to rent a car. I have found the buses of New Jersey to be cleaner than public transportation you would find in other parts of the country.

10. DO YOU NEED TO RENT A CAR?

This question does not have a simple answer. Where you stay, the duration of your stay, what sort of activities you are planning — those answers will determine whether you need to rent a car or not. New Jersey has accommodating public transportation and ride-sharing coverage is almost universal. You can get almost anywhere with an Uber or Lyft. From a population center, like Princeton, New Brunswick, Jersey City, etc., I would say you may not need to rent a vehicle for your stay in New Jersey. If you are staying at a bed and breakfast, potentially off the beaten path, I would suggest you rent a car. If you intend to go hiking or biking, renting a car is the best option and you should spend extra to rent an SUV. There are a number of excellent places to hike or bike, but they may be off the beaten path and may require a sturdy all-wheel drive vehicle. I like the freedom and flexibility renting a car provides, but I do not like how much renting a car can cost. This decision is ultimately yours to make and depends on how you wish to spend your time in New Jersey.

11. TRAVEL: HOTEL OR AIRBNB?

This is an interesting question I never used to consider when traveling. Whether or not a hotel or Airbnb makes sense for you will depend on a number of different circumstances. Where you stay in the state matters. There are a number of quaint, pretty little towns throughout New Jersey, but as I have already mentioned, smaller towns are not always optimized for public transportation. An array of attractive Airbnb locations are off the beaten path; not in sketchy areas but in less populated areas. Airbnb reviews have been pretty accurate all over the country, in my experience, and I have not heard too many horror stories about Airbnb stays in New Jersey. Also consider how you plan to eat. I prefer to mix it up, with home cooked meals and restaurant trips. If you want to visit New Jersey but you are not interested in trying the local food scene, Airbnb is the way to go. If you are looking to stay in a town and want to dine out for every meal, a hotel experience is likely the better option. This is a personal choice you will make for yourself.

12. FOOD: DOWNLOAD LOCAL EATS

This tip alone justifies the purchase price of this book. Local Eats is a crowd-sourced restaurant review app which gives you a quick rundown of the best places to eat within a pre-set radius of a few miles. The app can be incredibly useful but it has drawbacks. I have been in areas of the country where the 'local eats' were terrible. The recommendations are only as good as the people who are ratings restaurants. I have absolutely been in cities or towns which steered me wrong, with every local eats recommendation worse than the last. Bad recommendations is not my experience with the app in New Jersey, a state with a competitive food scene and a large, diverse population. I found a number of great places to eat, many off the beaten path, using Local Eats. Just before I moved out of New Jersey, I found a great diner in an area of Trenton I never would have visited otherwise. You can use Local Eats with complete confidence in the state of New Jersey.

13. FOOD: TRY TO FIND A FARMERS MARKET OR ROADSIDE VEGETABLE STAND

People from outside of New Jersey are almost always surprised by the availability, quality and quantity of fresh produce. The Garden State produces a surprising amount of fresh foods. There are a number of high quality farmers markets throughout the state. I am mostly familiar with the one in Trenton. There are also a number of 'roadside' farmers stands, outside of farms, which have fresh produce available. Farmers market prices are not only competitive but cheaper than what you would find in a grocery store. Vegetable stands have a wide range of quality and prices. If you find yourself at a farmers market, be sure to shop around before purchasing anything. You might find better quality at lower prices just around the corner or at the other end of the area. Of course, you should be discerning. A little ugliness in a fresh grown vegetable is fine. If the vegetables look like a facsimile drawn by a five year old who lacks artistic talent, just walk away. This isn't a fairy tale. Sometimes the ugly duckling grows up to be an ugly duck. Don't be a hero; hookworm treatments are expensive!

14. FOOD: ON SANDWICHES (AND BURGERS)

You have already missed the glory days of America's best sandwich. The Grease Trucks were a New Brunswick staple for years. Maxim magazine listed the Fat Darrell as America's #1 sandwich in 2004. Sports Illustrated named eating at the Grease Trucks as college football's #1 post-game activity. The Grease Trucks have moved, sadly, but find one if you can — their food is fantastic. You will find a number of 'hoagie' or 'sandwich' shops in New Jersey, but many of them are lackluster. Hoagie Haven in Princeton is an exception, as are the aforementioned Grease Trucks of New Brunswick, if you can find them. If you are in the mood, check Local Eats for your best options. I encourage you to find a Fat Darrell if you can — they're amazing. Do you enjoy burgers? New Jersey has a few excellent burger joints. Bobby Flay's Burger Palace in Lawrenceville makes fantastic food. White Manna in Hackensack and Zinburger at multiple locations are also great options. There are a few 'chain' burger joints to choose, as well — Five Guys, Moo-Yah, Smashburger and The Habit are examples. Of those, Five Guys is probably the best, followed by Moo-

Yah; I was unimpressed by both Smashburger and
The Habit, though your tastes might be different.

15. FOOD: PORK ROLL IS FANTASTIC

Similar to Canadian bacon, yet subtly different,
pork roll is a food which is almost uniquely found in
New Jersey. I do not understand why this form of
processed pork has not spread throughout the entire
country. Pork roll is delicious! Everyone I know who
has moved out of New Jersey pines for pork roll.
Well cooked pork roll is salty, savory with a hint of
spice and pork roll should be a little charred for a
slight snappiness. Taylor Ham is the original form of
pork roll and remains the most popular brand of pork
roll. Taylor Ham is also by far the most expensive
pork roll! Taylor Ham has great quality, but so do its
lower cost competitors. When I lived in New Jersey, I
tried different pork roll brands. Whenever I visit New
Jersey now I only buy Taylor Ham so I am certain of
what I am getting. Since all grocery stores carry
different pork roll brands you should always check
online to see if the lower cost brands are worth
buying. Sometimes, you can find a value. Sometimes,

you get what you pay for. The Porkroll Connection is another high quality choice.

16. FOOD: DINERS

You can find diners almost anywhere, but you will find a ton of diners in New Jersey. Diners are frequently open 24/7 and they usually have a wide selection of different foods for you to choose from. There are no major 'diner chains' which I am aware of, unless you consider chains such as IHOP or Perkins to be diners. There are two basic varieties of diners in New Jersey: standard diners and Greek diners. Food quality, service quality and cleanliness vary from diner to diner, sometimes varying widely from night to night at the same location! It is not unusual to find teenagers hanging out in a diner at later hours, as they have little else to do until they turn twenty-one. Never judge a book by its cover: the best diner I found in the state was in sketchy looking place in the midst of a run-down neighborhood in Trenton. The food and beer was cheap and you could not ask for better breakfast sausage. If you have never tried a diner before, New Jersey might be the best place to give it a shot!

17. FOOD: ALMOST ANY PIZZA IS GOOD

Once upon a time, I found myself in an unfamiliar area while traveling north on Route 1. This was in the dark ages, roughly 2006 or so and I did not have GPS on my flip-phone. While driving in the unfamiliar area, I saw a sign by a strip mall for pizza. I pulled in, stopped at the pizza place and ended up blown away by how good it was. Pizza is serious business in New York and New Jersey. There are pizza places all over. Any pizza place which has managed to stay open gets customers, and as competitive as it is in NJ, you only get customers by making great pizza. Long story short? You can walk into virtually any pizza place in NJ and get a better pizza than you'd get anywhere outside of the Philadelphia, NJ and NYC area. Don't hesitate to walk into a random pizza place and place an order: you'll love it. My personal favorites are the thin crust experts, such as Federici's in Freehold, DeLorenzo's in Robbinsville and Conte's in Princeton. A small disclaimer: I worked for my father's company for a time and my father did for Conte's. My father worked at a lot of restaurants, however, and Conte's is the only one getting a mention.

18. FOOD: INDIAN FOOD

The population of New Jersey has a lot of ethnic representation. Among the largest ethnic groups in New Jersey is Indian immigrants. With over 290,000 Indian-American residents, New Jersey has the third largest Indian-American population in the country, and by far the most Indian-American density per square mile of any location outside of India. There may be a few exceptional Indian restaurants throughout the country, but no state offers the sheer plethora of available Indian food the way New Jersey does. There are a number of great Indian places along the NE Corridor line: Trenton, Hamilton, Princeton, New Brunswick Edison, Rahway, Metuchen, etc. My favorite Indian restaurant was just outside of Lawrenceville, but I am not sure if it is still open. As always, check the Local Eats app or search online for reviews.

19. FOOD: WEGMAN'S IS BETTER THAN WHOLE FOODS

If you end up staying at an Airbnb you might end up going grocery shopping to cook at the location and save a little money. Shoprite, Acme and Stop 'N Shop are popular stores in the state. You can find Walmart and Target locations with grocery options, as well. ALDI and Trader Joe's operate around the state and both have low-cost food but an inconsistent selection. The biggest and fanciest options are Whole Foods, a national chain, and Wegman's, a regional grocery chain. I have expressed my feelings in the title. Wegman's is the best large grocery store I have ever been in. The produce is fresh, the organic section is robust and many locations have an in-house liquor store. Wegman's store-brand products are good, especially non-food items such as coffee. To be fair, Whole Foods has the best vanilla New York style cheesecake I have ever found in a grocery store. There are BJ's, Sam's Club and Costco locations all over the state and they all offer great prices, but buying in bulk might not be the best option if you are only instate for a few days.

20. FOOD: MICROBREWERIES

Microbreweries have popped up all over the country over the past few years. Many microbreweries have adjoined restaurants which offer upscale food options. Many of my favorite microbreweries are in the state of New Jersey. I may have gone to Triumph Brewery at least once a month when I lived in Princeton. The food is really good and I always enjoyed their beer flight sampler. Triumph is in Princeton and has Princeton prices. The Harvest Moon brewery in New Brunswick was another of my favorite places to go, moreso after Uber and Lyft gained popularity. I found the beers more enjoyable than the food at Harvest Moon, but it is still a fun environment with a fun atmosphere. If you are just looking for a beer, Carton brewery in Atlantic Highlands receives high praise for their use of ingredients. The Kane Brewing Company in Ocean Township has also gained national attention for their craft beers and 'brunch' beers. Remember to drive safe and use a designated driver or ride-sharing program when drinking!

21. FOOD: BE CAUTIOUS WITH SEAFOOD

Coastal states are renowned for their fresh seafood and seafood culture. I've found New Jersey to be a mixed bag regarding seafood. A lot of the best fish head to New York, not New Jersey. Pricing pressure limits the quality of available seafood for a number of restaurants. There are a number of great seafood restaurants, of course, but the issue is value. It is expensive to operate a restaurant in New Jersey, especially with a liquor license, so prices will either be high or the quality low. The shore towns of southern New Jersey are an exception as they receive fresh fish caught off the southern tip of the state. Further north, BYOB locations may be your best bet for good seafood at reasonable prices. If price is not an issue for you, you can find great seafood all over the state. If price is an issue, consider buying fresh seafood from a grocery store or skipping seafood altogether. Also, this rule applies to restaurants which specialize in seafood; you can get really good seafood options at steakhouses, Mediterranean restaurants, etc.

22. ATTRACTIONS: THEATERS

In many states, the theaters or venues cluster together in one area, such as Broadway in New York or the Theater District in London. There is no single population center in New Jersey, so theaters are spread throughout the state as a result. The Prudential Center, home of the New Jersey Devils, has a capacity of 19,500 and hosts large scale events such as concerts and comedy shows; the PNC Bank Arts Center similarly hosts large events and has a capacity of 17,500. Both venues are easily accessible and have a number of concession options but they are expensive. I won't lie, I was never interested in dinner theater, so I had to solicit other opinions. The Hunterdon Hills Playhouse received praise for its comfort, accessibility and acoustics, so if you are into dinner theater, this might be an option. A lot of excellent comedians come through the Stress Factory, the state's best dedicated comedy club, located in New Brunswick. A few other notable theaters are the State Theater in New Brunswick, the New Jersey Performing Arts Center in Newark, the Bergen Performing Arts Center in Englewood and the Wellmont Theater in Montclair.

23. ATTRACTIONS: HIKING AND BIKING

New Jersey has amazing hiking and biking paths. I grew up on the Sourland mountains, so I cannot claim an unbiased opinion. The Sourland Mountain Preserve hiking trails were only three miles from my childhood home. Since I was so close to the Preserve, I did not travel to many of the other hiking trails, but I can say Hemlock Falls and Hemlock Pond, located in Walpack, are fantastic. You can look up other 'top choices' online; hiking trails are a dime a dozen in the state. Try to locate trails close to where you stay. There are plenty of biking trails for you to explore, as well. The Delaware and Raritan Canal State Park Trail is the closest to the Princeton area, which is where I suggest you stay when visiting New Jersey. A lot of the top rated trails are in Monmouth County, though, so you might check out multiple trails in one day if you are feeling up for it. In my experience, the trails are busiest in the summer and on the weekends. If you can find time to hit the trails at roughly mid-morning on a random Tuesday, you should find the trails unoccupied.

24. ATTRACTIONS: WATER ACTIVITIES

Similar to hiking and biking, New Jersey has a number of excellent places to canoe, kayak, go tubing, etc. Most of the water based activities center around a few areas, such as canoe rental shops in Princeton or the Pine Barrens. The Pine Barrens are, predictably, barren. The terrain is ugly and dull, in my opinion, but if you find pictures and disagree with me, go for it. Prices tend to be cheaper in the Pine Barrens than they are in the center or northern parts of the state. The Princeton Canoe Rental is right on the water and you can get to the Delaware and Raritan Canal, Stony Brook and Carnegie Lake. I have only kayaked the small snaking rivers of the area, while Carnegie Lake is described as the most popular tour. Tubing is a lot of fun and I would bet most people would love it. The Delaware River Tubing rental is in Milford, New Jersey and has affordable prices. People are surprised when the two hour tour is too short. This is a popular activity in New Jersey and you will see why if you attempt it.

25. ATTRACTIONS: SPORTING EVENTS

Let me get the biggest sports out of the way so you can learn about less popular (and better valued) choices. New Jersey is home to the New Jersey Devils in the NHL, as well as the New York Jets and New York Giants of the NFL. The New York Red Bull soccer team has their home stadium in Harrison, New Jersey. If you are interested, the NFL games are expensive and it is difficult to get out of the stadium unless you pay high prices for premium parking. Expect traffic leaving Met Life Stadium. The Devils are a competitive team and the stadium isn't too crowded unless it is a rivalry game. If you just want to catch a game, you might want to skip matchups with the NY Rangers or Philadelphia Flyers as the arena will be rowdy and full. The real value is in minor league teams: the Trenton Thunder and the Trenton Titans are two of the biggest. Both teams have accessible stadiums and a fun atmosphere. Better yet, you will find both ticket and concession prices to be reasonable. Unless you have a burning passion to see professional sports in New Jersey, you should focus more on catching a minor league game. Oh, what about college sports? Well, Rutgers is generally terrible at all of the sports. I have no further comment.

26. ATTRACTIONS: GROUNDS FOR SCULPTURE

I never had an interest in going to the Grounds for Sculpture in Hamilton until a friend encouraged me to come with them. The experience was impressive. The area is huge, with too many sculptures to see in one visit, unless you plan to be there all day. Exhibitions are always changing, so it is best to not get too deep into what I saw. The Grounds for Sculpture has six separate places to eat, and a number of special one-off events. Some of the exhibits are interactive. Some of them are gigantic in size. Overall the grounds cover 42 acres and hosts over 250 statues. The price for admission and concessions is reasonable. The only drawback is accessibility. Hamilton is a bit remote, limiting your options to get there via public transportation. Hail a taxi, Uber or Lyft to go. Grounds for Sculpture is among the most impressive art exhibits you will ever see.

27. ATTRACTIONS: FISHING AND HUNTING

Let me sum up my vast and expansive knowledge of hunting. People go into the woods and try to shoot things. My knowledge of hunting is concluded. In New Jersey, at certain points during the year, people are authorized to hunt bears. I have read articles about a few bear hunters who go off into the woods with nothing but a bow, some arrows and a dream. I think of these people and I wonder, "Do their mothers know?!" I know a lot more about fishing. There are a number of excellent fishing locations in New Jersey. You can find deep-sea fishing all over the coastal areas of the state. I have friends who go shark fishing off the coast at least twice a year. New Jersey has close to four-hundred (400!) freshwater sources where you can go fishing if you wish. You will need to purchase a seasonal fishing license unless you are 16 or younger. The license only costs $22.50 and it can be purchased at many sporting good stores, fishing rental locations or online from the New Jersey Division of Fish and Wildlife.

28. ATTRACTIONS: MUSEUMS AND AQUARIUM

For me, the best museum in New Jersey is the Liberty Science Center, located in Jersey City. Wikipedia describes it as, "…an interactive science museum and learning center…" which is fair, but cold. You can go there and do science stuff with interactive exhibits. Create lightning! Learn about skyscrapers! See different sources of energy at work! I want to say children will love it, but adults have a lot of fun there, too. The New Jersey State Museum of Trenton houses a number of artifacts from the history of the state, fine art and natural history. The Princeton University Art Museum, in Princeton, houses fine art from the university, state of New Jersey and beyond. The Adventure Aquarium in Camden is a great place to visit if you want to experience the wondrous scenery of underwater environments before you get murdered. I'm joking, of course — the aquarium is in the safest part of Camden. You'll still get shot, it just won't be as severe; the bullet will merely graze you, no biggie. Finally, the Red Mill Museum Village attraction is a favorite in the state. The mill still works and the village remains preserved from when the mill opened in the 1800's. There are a dozen or so historical buildings to tour. If you enjoy history, the Red Mill Museum Village might be the highlight of your trip.

29. ATTRACTIONS: AMUSEMENT PARKS

New Jersey has a wide selection of amusement parks. The biggest and most notable amusement park is Six Flags Great Adventure & Safari, the second largest amusement park in the world after Disney Animal Kingdom. Six Flags, located in Jackson, can be reached with public transportation. There are 11 themed areas in Six Flags which you can visit. Compared to Disney Land or Disney World, Six Flags usually has faster lines and cheaper prices.

The Safari park has live animals you can drive up to and visit with. If you have children, Six Flags might be a great option. Many of the shore towns also have amusement parks on their boardwalks. Wildwood's boardwalk is almost exclusively an amusement park. Atlantic City has an amusement park at Steel Pier. There are a number of Go-Kart and Mini-Golf locations all over the state — they tend to differ in name only. You can get the same half-decent chicken tenders and fries meal at almost all of them. If you have the time and the inclination, Six Flags is a lot of fun. I would also recommend spending time at Wildwood or Steel Pier if you are nearby and have children.

30. ATTRACTIONS: SHOPPING

Shopping for clothes in New Jersey is a viable vacation activity. New Jersey has a number of high-quality clothing outlets and no state sales tax on clothes. You can get good items at good prices and you will not have to pay taxes on them. It is a win/win/win scenario. A few outlets cluster together, such as the Jackson Premium Outlets which has close to 80 separate stores, including Adidas, Coach, J. Crew, New York & Company, Reebok and Zales. I grew up near the outlets in Flemington (Liberty Village) so I am familiar with them; I found myself at the outlets in Atlantic City for a brief moment once. You can certainly take a look at any of the available options if you are interested. If you end up buying a lot, weigh up whether it is cheaper to ship your new purchases home, rather than stuffing it in your luggage and potentially getting hit with a weight penalty on checked bags.

31. LOCATIONS: PRINCETON

I grew up right outside of Princeton and lived there for a while. I believe Princeton is among the nicest places in the country. If you are traveling to New Jersey, you should strongly consider using Princeton as a 'home base' for your trip. Without traffic, you can drive to Philadelphia in about an hour; you can drive to New York in about an hour and a half. Princeton has a local train-station called the "dinky" which connects to the Princeton-Junction train-station. From Princeton-Junction, you can either head south to Trenton and from there onto Philadelphia, or take the Northeast Corridor line up to New York City at Penn Station. The architecture is fascinating and you can wander around the open campus of Princeton University. The town itself is small, encompassing only a few blocks. Princeton is gorgeous in the summer, with rich greens everywhere, flowers in bloom and clean, well manicured streets. A lot of the 'locals' spend time away from Princeton in the summer, giving it a calm and tranquil feel. This is an upscale, wealthy area. Prices are high and stores stock premium goods. The restaurant scene is excellent. Budget-conscious travelers should stay near or outside of Princeton, in places such as Lawrenceville, Plainsboro or the Windsors.

32. LOCATIONS: ATLANTIC CITY

Atlantic City does not suit my taste. I'm not much of a gambler and I find some of the areas around Atlantic City a bit sad. There are plenty of things to do besides gambling. The Atlantic City boardwalk is famous, though a bit faded these days. There are plenty of family friendly activities on the boardwalk, including a small-scale amusement park at Steel Pier. There are carnival games and shorefront stores along the entirety of the boardwalk as well as casino entrances. Atlantic City is appropriate during 'family hours;' you won't find wild behavior until after dark. As it gets later, AC comes to life with a number of night clubs, bars, etc. Night clubs located at hotels can get downright scandalous. In my experience, the Borgata is the best hotel and casino in Atlantic City. Hotels and casinos of AC are not as upscale or attractive as their Las Vegas counterparts. Drive to Atlantic City if possible, as it tends to be the easiest way into town.

33. LOCATIONS: SMALL TOWNS

There are a number of unique, charming and interesting little towns scattered around New Jersey. A lot of the nicer areas of the state fall along the Northeast Corridor line, which goes from Trenton to New York City. Hopewell is a quiet little town with great dining options and a developing main street. Nearby Clinton has the highly popular Red Mill Museum Village. Mount Holly is a mixture of a modern town combined with a historic and visually stunning Main Street. Perhaps the nicest little town in the state is Lambertville and it's adjacent town in Pennsylvania, New Hope. Lambertville has a number of small artisan shops: art galleries, furniture stores, antique stores, clothing shops, etc. There are a number of fine dining options in Lambertville and New Hope, as well as cultural points of interest. I would say the dining options in Lambertville and New Hope were good but surprisingly pricey the last time I went, but the overall experience was well worth the cost.

34. LOCATIONS: COASTAL TOWNS

Coastal towns offer more than just a beach. Asbury Park is an example of a coastal town: it has beaches, sure, but it also has a lot of other things. Asbury Park has fine dining, cultural options and great entertainment. Asbury Park has undergone a number of improvements over the past twenty years or so and the town has made amazing progress as a result. I'm also fond of Red Bank, which is similar to Asbury Park. Red Bank can be downright sleepy at night, but it is a quiet and relaxing place to take a deep breath and relax. Brick is a town with a thriving artistic community. It takes a bit of effort to get to the water, from Brick, which may or may not disqualify it for some travelers. I was impressed with the town and found a number of interesting stores along the retail sector. Spring Lake is a wealthy coastal town with nice beaches, a beautiful lake and a number of really upscale dining and shopping options.

35. LOCATIONS: SHORE TOWNS

When it comes to the Jersey Shore, there are towns which are exclusively 'shore towns' — casual dining, the boardwalk, entertainment, the beach and nothing else. The real shore towns are places such as Cape May, Wildwood, Seaside Heights, Avalon, Ocean City and the whole of Long Beach Island. Cape May is family friendly and has incredible beaches, architecture and a lot of activities. Wildwood is a blast, with a number of attractions, a spirited boardwalk and great casual food choices. Avalon is a bit hipsterish for my tastes, but it gets great reviews from the Avocado Toast crowd. Seaside Heights is a bit of a mixed bag; though it has a number of family attractions and wholesome fun, the town gets rowdy; it was the location of the first season of Jersey Shore; it was not an accident. During the summer, it is not unusual to have a lot of drunk, aggressive college-aged people roaming around, looking for all forms of mischief. If you're into such a scene, Seaside Heights is great. If you've got kids and don't want to hide them after dark, maybe head to Cape May or Wildwood, instead.

36. LOCATIONS: COLLEGE TOWNS

College towns skew younger, tend to be more open-minded and have a more active night life. Major college towns are Brighton Avenue in West Long Branch, Hoboken, Montclair, Stockton and New Brunswick, the biggest of them all. West Long Branch is inland from Long Branch and it features a ton of nightlife options and easy access to the beach. Hoboken is a fast developing New York suburb which has trendy eating, art, music and upscale drinking options. Stockton is a bit more rural, but still has a number of really interesting food and drink options, as well as a vibrant college community which enjoys itself. New Brunswick is a burgeoning city which rivals any 'campus town' in the country. New Brunswick has night clubs, fine dining, upscale bars and the Stress Factory, a popular comedy club. If you are looking for the college town vibe, any of these towns will fit your needs. I do not consider Princeton a college town because it is quiet, sleepy and lacks a proper night life. Princeton students usually drive to New Brunswick when they're looking to party.

37. LOCATIONS: NEWARK / JERSEY CITY

Newark was once a glistening city which had an excellent reputation. Much of the city faced serious strife during race riots which occurred after Martin Luther King Jr's assassination. This once proud city has not recovered from those troubles nearly sixty years ago. Jersey City is similar. There are upscale parts of both cities, such as Ironbound section of Newark and the Downtown, Newport and Paulus Hook areas of Jersey City. Both Newark and Jersey City have issues with crime, so be careful where you go. Both Jersey City and Newark are improving as people choose lower-cost alternatives to New York City. You can easily travel from either if you want to head into NYC. Public transportation is abundant in both. You can stay in either Newark or Jersey City and spend your entire trip in NYC; it takes less than a half hour to get from either to New York. Jersey City has a PATH station which will take you right to the Wall Street area. Newark Penn Station is connected to New York Penn Station.

38. LOCATIONS: CAMDEN

Once upon a time, a friend of mine told me a joke which still makes me laugh: "Detroit went to Camden. Detroit got stabbed. Detroit never even made it off the bus." News articles about Camden frequently remark on how much safer Camden is becoming! Apparently the likelihood of you getting shot has decreased to to a mere 88%! Such statistics might be an exaggeration, but this is not: Camden is legitimately dangerous. The potential dangers include being mugged, robbed, assaulted, carjacked or even murdered! Even the 'safe places' in Camden are not as safe as they should be. The Adventure Aquarium is safe, as are the Rutgers-Camden dorms. Downtown Camden and the office parks nearby are safe-ish, but not a lot of territory is considered 'safe' for a city of 300,000+. I live in Chicago and I walk around at night without concern. I wouldn't feel safe driving through Camden in a tank at high noon. I cannot stress this enough: do not go to Camden.

39. LOCATION: DAY TRIP TO NEW YORK

What advice do I have for those of you traveling to New York City? First and foremost, take the train. There is no traffic which compares to a backed up New York City, not even Los Angeles. You can probably get to New York on a round-trip ticket for around $20 or so using NJ Transit. Next, plan ahead and make sure you have reservations or tickets before you get to New York. You do not need to reserve tickets for museums or galleries, but you do need to book tickets for live events. If you are planning on having drinks in the city, make sure you have a designated driver. Restaurants in New York are more expensive than anywhere else in the country. Drinks are more expensive than anywhere else in the country. If you are going to experience fine dining, dress for the occasion. There is more to do in New York than you could accomplish in a day or a weekend, so try to plan ahead, as much as you can, so you can capitalize on your time there. New York is much safer than it used to be, but you should still exercise caution.

40. LOCATION: DAY TRIP TO PHILADELPHIA

Philadelphia is far more car friendly than New York. The city layout is mostly optimized to help ease congestion and traffic. Taking a car into Philadelphia is not as awful as driving in New York, but finding parking can be difficult and expensive. Philadelphia is a huge city with a beautiful downtown section. The outer suburbs can be rough, so avoid them. Philadelphia has a number of fascinating museums, including the Franklin Institute and Philadelphia Museum of Art. Philadelphia is home to sports franchises in the NFL, NBA, MLB and NHL, as well as a soccer team… if you're into that sort of thing. There are a number of excellent fine dining establishments, such as Vetri and Le Virtù. DiNic's Roast Pork in Philadelphia's Reading Terminal Market has been rated among the best sandwiches in America. Philadelphia's Chinatown has some excellent restaurants. Walk from store to store and restaurant to restaurant in Chinatown. I highly recommend the Shanghai Soup Dumplings from Dim Sum Garden. There is a wait whenever you go there, but their food is worth it.

41. NJ CULTURE: GAS STATIONS ARE FULL SERVICE!

To the best of my knowledge, New Jersey is the only state in America which mandates full service gas stations. At a full service station, someone pumps the gas for you — it is their job. You could attempt to exit your car and attempt to the reach the pumps before the attendant, but rules prohibit you from doing so. Just relax and let the attendants do their job! There is no need to jump out of your car to pump gas in New Jersey. The full service gas station rules were enacted because gas theft was a common practice once. If you choose to jump out and pump your own gas, expect poor treatment from the attendant. When it comes to tipping, you do not need to tip the gas station attendant. Attendants do not expect gratuities, so do not feel put upon to give one. If the attendant goes out of their way to help you, such as cleaning your windshield without prompting, consider giving them a tip.

42. NJ CULTURE: TICKS!

New Jersey has a surprising amount of uncultured land, which can give you scenic views and peaceful moments of reflection. The uncultured land can also give you a nasty case of Lyme disease. Lyme disease is an exploding issue for New Jersey, diagnosed more than 5,000 times in 2017. Lyme disease comes from deer ticks, a tiny species of tick which are almost imperceptible to the naked eye. Lyme disease causes lethargy, rashes, joint pain, meningitis, facial paralysis, nausea and vomiting. If you are staying in wooded areas use bug spray — I have had success with Off! Deep Wood. Whenever possible, wear long pants and long sleeves, full shoes with socks and avoid the thick brush or similar areas. Lyme disease can strike with any tick bite, so exercise caution. If you think this is only an issue for wooded areas, please know that Camden county saw over 1,000 recorded cases of Lyme disease since 2000. Just remember, you can get shot anywhere, but only in Camden can you get shot and bitten by an infected tick at the same time.

43. NJ CULTURE: DO NOT FEED DEER!

For work purposes, I would find myself at houses all over the state. At one house near a wooded area, I noticed a family of deer. There is nothing unusual about seeing deer, but they did not appear afraid of me. I noticed one of the deer had a bow wrapped around its neck. I was able to ask the owner of the property about it and the owner told me they had left food out for the deer. After a while, the deer had become comfortable around the owner (and family) while also becoming more comfortable around all people, as well. The owner spoke with pride, implying it was a triumph. I cannot stress this enough: deer are wild animals, and though they tend to be harmless, they are not pets. Do not feed deer. Domesticating a deer makes them less reliant on their own natural food gathering techniques and weakens their chance for long term survival. The younger deer were not being taught how to survive, they were being taught how to receive food from humans. What happens to those deer if the owners of the property move away or stop feeding them? Worse, what happens if another animal shows up and starts taking the food? Want to know what else might swing by your backyard if you leave food out there? Bears.

44. NJ CULTURE: BEARS. REALLY.

New Jersey is the state with the highest population density. New Jersey is nicknamed The Garden State, for justifiable reasons. Close to 17% of the land is agricultural. There are state parks and nature preserves all over the state. That natural bounty provides New Jersey with breathtaking views, amazing scenic hiking trails… and bears. New Jersey has a stunning amount of bears. More than 1,000 bears are roaming around in the wild, according to expert estimates. Every county in New Jersey has a confirmed bear sighting since 2012. New Jersey is home to black bears, a mostly peaceful breed of bear that does not attack humans unless they are directly attacked or a bear cub is perceived to be endangered by a human. That is the good news. Black bears can literally rip a human's arms off. That is the bad news. Bears are becoming more conditioned to treat humans as a food source as they scavenge through trash and refuse to find nourishment. Black bears are excellent climbers and can chase you up a tree. They can outrun you. If they attack you, they can be lethal. Black bears are much safer to encounter than grizzly bears or mountain lions, but they are still extremely dangerous. If you are staying at a home, lock your trash up and never engage a black bear.

45. NJ CULTURE: BOARDWALKS

I did not realize how rare boardwalks were until I realized how few of them there are anywhere else in America. Almost every beach community in New Jersey has a boardwalk, though some are more popular than others. A proper New Jersey boardwalk should have a fair or carnival atmosphere, with games, attractions, casual dining and shops. You may enjoy strolling along boardwalks, since the walk is not too long and the atmosphere is lively. Fancier or more elaborate boardwalks have ferris wheels, amusement parks and rides. Atlantic City's Garden Pier is a fascinating spot which attracts top musical and entertainment acts. The boardwalk of Wildwood is practically its own amusement park without an admission price. For food, grab a funnel cake or a giant slice of thin-crust pizza and wash it down with a soda. Boardwalks are not unique to New Jersey, as you can find them in Chicago, Santa Monica, Virginia Beach and Myrtle Beach, etc. If you are in New Jersey and find yourself at a beach, though, take a moment to look for the boardwalks.

46. NJ CULTURE: WAWA AND QUICKCHEK

Over the years I have realized a few fundamental truths about the world. You can always find a McDonalds or CVS. There are Dunkin' Donuts on almost every street corner of Massachusetts. Hardees and Sonic are actual restaurants in the southeast, as opposed to mere commercials; I discovered In-N-Out Burger in San Diego. Other than 7-11 and Circle K, convenience stores are mostly regional; not even 7-11 or Circle K have stores in every state. New Jersey has two strong competitors for the best convenience store: Wawa and Quickchek. Both sell fresh food of a higher quality than you might expect. Both have integrated gas stations at many locations. Both sell reasonably priced sodas, chips and snacks. Of the two, Wawa is perceived by many to be the superior choice. Wawa Hoagies (subs, submarines, heroes, grinders) are a popular lunch choice and both stores are very busy at lunch time. These are not five-star, can't miss eateries, but in a pinch, either is a safe place to find a bite to eat. Neither convenience store has great coffee, though.

47. NJ CULTURE: BUY LIQUOR AT LIQUOR STORES

If you are not from New Jersey, you are in for a rude awakening when you try to find a six-pack at your local convenience store. New Jersey is a state which does not allow liquor sales in a number of store types, such as grocery stores and convenience stores. Trader Joe's and Wegman's are the only grocery stores which sell liquor in the whole state, to my knowledge. I have no idea why you cannot buy liquor in grocery stores in New Jersey. Specialty stores that only sell liquor, or mostly sell liquor, exist across the state. Blue laws prohibiting the sale alcohol on Sunday's do exist in some areas; There is a large variation in prices at different liquor stores across the state. Common sense can help you determine the best places to buy your alcohol. Princeton shops have expertly curated wine and liquor selections and the prices, as you might imagine, are high. Venture outside of the upscale areas if you want to buy liquor as you could end up saving a few dollars for every purchase you make. Not a few dollars total, mind you, but a few dollars per item. There are parts of New Jersey with price points similar to New York City. Try to avoid them whenever you can.

48. NJ CULTURE: WEIRD NJ LOCATIONS ARE DISAPPOINTING

I am not sure if the 'Weird America' series is still going strong, but I do remember it gained popularity when I was younger. Weird NJ came out when I was in high school and it was exciting! Danger! Mystery! Intrigue! Man, what a let down when we could drive cars and started visiting these places. I found out one of these 'weird and spooky locations' was right down the street from where I lived, less than a quarter of a mile away. Weird and spooky? I knew the family which lived across the street! The family across the street was so boring they were otherwise unremarkable! Similar disappointments lurked at each and every one of these locations.

• The Devil's Tree: Literally a tree. The tree does not move, talk or come to life. The tree behaves in a manner befitting a tree, i.e., it does nothing. What a complete and total waste of time.

• Clinton Road in West Milford: It's a road. No ghosts, goblins or gremlins; asphalt and roadsigns. Total waste of time.

• Gingerbread Castle Road: Not only is this boring to look at, the location is dangerous. The amusement park is rotting and structurally unsound. It is falling apart and people wind up injured wandering around every year.

You want scares? During the fall, try the Field of Terror corn maze in East Windsor. It is a fantastic experience. Sure, the fear is real, even if the frights that inspire them are not. Fictional fear is better than boredom. Weird NJ locations are real and come with the painful mundaneness reality tends to imbue.

49. NJ CULTURE: YOU CAN DO A SOPRANO'S OR JERSEY SHORE TOUR!

Don't. I could leave it there, but you might want more details. The Soprano's was a great show because it was realistic. Week in and week out, you saw the life of a mid-level crime boss as he went about his daily routine. The real driving force of the show was its realism and the grittiness which the criminal lifestyle entailed. Soprano tours and mafia tours are dull, in my opinion. Satriale's is one of the most iconic locations from the show but it was demolished in 2007. As for the Jersey Shore, the 'tour' consists of seeing the house where the cast stayed during their first season. Maybe these activities appeal to you, but they do not appeal to me. If you are visiting New Jersey, there are a number of activities to do, places to see and foods to sample — don't waste your time on the Soprano's or Jersey Shore!

50. NJ CULTURE: OH! YOU TALKIN' TO ME?! FUGHETABOUIT!

Yes, I lived in New Jersey for most of my adult life and I know the stereotype people have in their heads. I won't delve into diversity statistics or anything, just know New Jersey is far more than Italian immigrants. As to the specific stereotype of New Jersey as a mobbed up den of thieves... well, I'd love to tell you it is a completely overblown trope and a work of complete fiction. I lived in New Brunswick, however, and I know a guy. I went to a house party he hosted once, and I met a bunch of his friends — the guys he knows. You can hardly throw a rock in New Jersey without hitting someone who knows a guy, or the guy who knows the guy, or worse, if you threw the rock, the guy himself! Organized crime exists everywhere, it's just more public in New Jersey. The most dangerous types of criminals are desperate people with nothing to lose. When it comes to the mafia in New Jersey, you wouldn't know the genuine article if you met them. Of course, there are wannabe tough-guys in every corner of every state, and they can cause problems if you are not careful.

TOP REASONS TO BOOK THIS TRIP

Versatility: New Jersey offers mountain hiking, beach vacations, river rafting and all points in between. You can basically book three vacations but stay in one hotel or AirBnB

Location: New Jersey is in the heart of one of the world's largest metropolitan areas. You can easily get to New York City or Philadelphia.

Food: New Jersey offers a diverse selection of food choices. Few locations can offer similar access to excellent foods.

BONUS BOOK

50 THINGS TO KNOW ABOUT PACKING LIGHT FOR TRAVEL

PACK THE RIGHT WAY EVERY TIME

AUTHOR: MANIDIPA BHATTACHARYYA

Edited by Melanie Howthorne

ABOUT THE AUTHOR

Manidipa Bhattacharyya is a creative writer and editor, with an education in English literature and Linguistics. After working in the IT industry for seven long years she decided to call it quits and follow her heart instead. Manidipa has been ghost writing, editing, proof reading and doing secondary research services for many story tellers and article writers for about three years. She stays in Kolkata, India with her husband and a busy two year old. In her own time Manidipa enjoys travelling, photography and writing flash fiction.

Manidipa believes in travelling light and never carries anything that she couldn't haul herself on a trip. However, travelling with her child changed the scenario. She seemed to carry the entire world with her for the baby on the first two trips. But good sense prevailed and she is again working her way to becoming a light traveler, this time with a kid.

INTRODUCTION

He who would travel happily
must travel light.

-Antoine de Saint-Exupéry

Travel takes you to different places from seas and mountains to deserts and much more. In your travels you get to interact with different people and their cultures. You will, however, enjoy the sights and interact positively with these new people even more, if you are travelling light.

When you travel light your mind can be free from worry about your belongings. You do not have to spend precious vacation time waiting for your luggage to arrive after a long flight. There is be no chance of your bags going missing and the best part is that you need not pay a fee for checked baggage.

People who have mastered this art of packing light will root for you to take only one carry-on, wherever you go. However, many people can find it really hard to pack light. More so if you are travelling with children. Differentiating between "must have" and "just in case" items is the starting point. There will be ample shopping avenues at your destination which are just waiting to be explored.

This book will show you 'packing' in a new 'light' – pun intended – and help you to embrace light packing practices for all of your future travels.

Off to packing!

DEDICATION

I dedicate this book to all the travel buffs that I know, who have given me great insights into the contents of their backpacks.

THE RIGHT TRAVEL GEAR

1. CHOOSE YOUR TRAVEL GEAR CAREFULLY

While selecting your travel gear, pick items that are light weight, durable and most importantly, easy to carry. There are cases with wheels so you can drag them along – these are usually on the heavy side because of the trolley. Alternatively a backpack that you can carry comfortably on your back, or even a duffel bag that you can carry easily by hand or sling across your body are also great options. Whatever you choose, one thing to keep in mind is that the luggage itself should not weigh a ton, this will give you the flexibility to bring along one extra pair of shoes if you so desire.

2. CARRY THE MINIMUM NUMBER OF BAGS

Selecting light weight luggage is not everything. You need to restrict the number of bags you carry as well. One carry-on size bag is ideal for light travel. Most carriers allow one cabin baggage plus one purse, handbag or camera bag as long as it slides under the seat in front. So technically, you can carry two items of luggage without checking them in.

3. PACK ONE EXTRA BAG

Always pack one extra empty bag along with your essential items. This could be a very light weight duffel bag or even a sturdy tote bag which takes up minimal space. In the event that you end up buying a lot of souvenirs, you already have a handy bag to stuff all that into and do not have to spend time hunting for an appropriate bag.

I'm very strict with my packing and have everything in its right place. I never change a rule. I hardly use anything in the hotel room. I wheel my own wardrobe in and that's it.

Charlie Watts

CLOTHES & ACCESSORIES

4. PLAN AHEAD

Figure out in advance what you plan to do on your trip. That will help you to pick that one dress you need for the occasion. If you are going to attend a wedding then you have to carry formal wear. If not, you can ditch the gown for something lighter that will be comfortable during long walks or on the beach.

5. WEAR THAT JACKET

Remember that wearing items will not add extra luggage for your air travel. So wear that bulky jacket that you plan to carry for your trip. This saves space and can also help keep you warm during the chilly flight.

6. MIX AND MATCH

Carry clothes that can be interchangeably used to reinvent your look. Find one top that goes well with a couple of pairs of pants or skirts. Use tops, shirts and jackets wisely along with other accessories like a scarf or a stole to create a new look.

7. CHOOSE YOUR FABRIC WISELY

Stuffing clothes in cramped bags definitely takes its toll which results in wrinkles. It is best to carry wrinkle free, synthetic clothes or merino tops. This will eliminate the need for that small iron you usually bring along.

8. DITCH CLOTHES PACK UNDERWEAR

Pack more underwear and socks. These are the things that will give you a fresh feel even if you do not get a chance to wear fresh clothes. Moreover these are easy to wash and can be dried inside the hotel room itself.

9. CHOOSE DARK OVER LIGHT

While picking your clothes choose dark coloured ones. They are easy to colour coordinate and can last longer before needing a wash. Accidental food spills and dirt from the road are less visible on darker clothes.

10. WEAR YOUR JEANS

Take only one pair of Jeans with you, which you should wear on the flight. Remember to pick a pair that can be worn for sightseeing trips and is equally eloquent for dinner. You can add variety by adding light weight cargoes and chinos.

11. CARRY SMART ACCESSORIES

The right accessory can give you a fresh look even with the same old dress. An intelligent neck-piece, a couple of bright scarves, stoles or a sarong can be used in a number of ways to add variety to your clothing. These light weight beauties can double up as a nursing cover, a light blanket, beach wear, a modesty cover for visiting places of worship, and also makes for an enthralling game of peek-a-boo.

12. LEARN TO FOLD YOUR GARMENTS

Seasoned travellers all swear by rolling their clothes for compact and wrinkle free packing. Bundle packing, where you roll the clothes around a central object as if tying it up, is also a popular method of compact and wrinkle free packing. Stacking folded clothes one on top of another is a big no-no as it makes creases extreme and they are difficult to get rid of without ironing.

13. WASH YOUR DIRTY LAUNDRY

One of the ways to avoid carrying loads of clothes is to wash the clothes you carry. At some places you might get to use the laundry services or a Laundromat but if you are in a pinch, best solution is to wash them yourself. If that is the plan then carrying quick drying clothes is highly recommended, which most often also happen to be the wrinkle free variety.

14. LEAVE THOSE TOWELS BEHIND

Regular towels take up a lot of space, are heavy and take ages to dry out. If you are staying at hotels they will provide you with towels anyway. If you are travelling to a remote place, where the availability of towels look doubtful, carry a light weight travel towel of viscose material to do the job.

15. USE A COMPRESSION BAG

Compression bags are getting lots of recommendation now days from regular travellers. These are useful for saving space in your luggage when you have to pack bulky dresses. While packing for the return trip, get help from the hotel staff to arrange a vacuum cleaner.

FOOTWEAR

16. PUT ON YOUR HIKING BOOTS

If you have plans to go hiking or trekking during your trip, you will need those bulky hiking boots. The best way to carry them is to wear them on flight to save space and luggage weight. You can remove the boots once inside and be comfortable in your socks.

17. PICKING THE RIGHT SHOES

Shoes are often the bulkiest items, along with being the dainty if you are a female. They need care and take up a lot of space in your luggage. It is advisable therefore to pick shoes very carefully. If you plan to do a lot of walking and site seeing, then wearing a pair of comfortable walking shoes are a must. For more formal occasions you can carry durable, light weight flats which will not take up much space.

18. STUFF SHOES

If you happen to pack a pair of shoes, ensure you utilize their hollow insides. Tuck small items like rolled up socks or belts to save space. They will also be easy to find.

TOILETRIES

19. STASHING TOILETRIES

Carry only absolute necessities. Airline rules dictate that for one carry-on bag, liquids and gels must be in 3.4 ounce (100ml) bottles or less, and must be packed in a one quart zip-lock bag. If you are planning to stay in a hotel, the basic things will be provided for you. It's best is to buy the rest from the local market at your destination.

20. TAKE ALONG TAMPONS

Tampons are a hard to find item in a lot of countries. Figure out how many you need and pack accordingly. For longer stays you can buy them online and have them delivered to where you are staying.

21. GET PAMPERED BEFORE YOU TRAVEL

Some avid travellers suggest getting a pedicure and manicure just the day before travelling. This not only gives you a well kept look, you also save the trouble of packing nail polish. Remember, every little bit of weight reduced adds up.

ELECTRONICS

22. LUGGING ALONG ELECTRONICS

Electronics have a large role to play in our lives today. Most of us cannot imagine our lives away from our phones, laptops or tablets. However while travelling, one must consider the amount of weight these electronics add to our luggage. Thankfully smart phones come along with all the essentials tools like a camera, email access, picture editing tools and more. They are smart to the point of eliminating the need to carry multiple gadgets. Choose a smart phone that suits all your requirements and travel with the world in your palms or pocket.

23. REDUCE THE NUMBER OF CHARGERS

If you do travel with multiple electronic devices, you will have to bear the additional burden of carrying all their chargers too. Check if a single charger can be used for multiple devices. You might also consider investing in a pocket charger. These small devices support multiple devices while keeping you charged on the go.

24. TRAVEL FRIENDLY APPS

Along with smart phones come numerous apps, which are immensely helpful in our travels. You name it and you have an app for it at hand – take pictures, sharing with friends and family, torch to light dark roads, maps, checking flight/train times, find hotels and many other things. Use these smart alternatives to traditional items like books to eliminate weight and save space.

I get ideas about what's essential when packing my suitcase.

-Diane von Furstenberg

TRAVELLING WITH KIDS

25. BRING ALONG THE STROLLER

Kids might enjoy walking for a while but they soon tire out and a stroller is the just the right thing for them to rest in while you continue your tour. Strollers also double duty as a luggage carrier and shopping bag holder. Remember to pick a light weight, easy to handle brand of stroller. Better yet, find out in advance if you can rent a stroller at your destination.

26. BRING ONLY ENOUGH DIAPERS FOR YOUR TRIP

Diapers take up a lot of space and add to the weight of your luggage. Therefore it is advisable to carry just enough diapers to last through the trip and a few for afterwards, till you buy fresh stock at your destination. Unless of course you are travelling to a really remote area, in which case you have no choice but to carry the load. Otherwise diapers are something you will find pretty easily.

27. TAKE ONLY A COUPLE OF TOYS

Children are easily attracted by new things in their environment. While travelling they will find numerous 'new' objects to scrutinize and play with. Packing just one favorite toy is enough, or if there is no favorite toy leave out all of them in favor of stories or imaginary games.

28. CARRY KID FRIENDLY SNACKS

Create a small snack counter in your bag to store away quick bites for those sudden hunger pangs. Depending on the child's age this could include chocolates, raisins, dry fruits, granola bars or biscuits. Also keep a bottle of water handy for your little one.

These things do not add much weight and can be adjusted in a handbag or knapsack.

29. GAMES TO CARRY

Create some travel specific, imaginary games if you have slightly grown up children, like spot the attractions. Keep a coloring book and colors handy for in-flight or hotel time. Apps on your smart phone can keep the children engaged with cartoons and story books. Older children are often entertained by games available on phones or tablets. This cuts the weight of luggage down while keeping the kids entertained.

30. LET THE KIDS CARRY THEIR LOAD

A good thing is to start early sharing of responsibilities. Let your child pick a bag of his or her choice and pack it themselves. Keep tabs on what they are stuffing in their bags by asking if they will be using that item on the trip. It could start out being just an entertainment bag initially but with growing years they will learn to sort the useful from the superfluous. Children as little as four can maneuver a small trolley suitcase like a pro- their experience in pull along toys credit. If you are worried that you may be pulling it for them, you may want to start with a backpack.

31. DECIDE ON LOCATION FOR CHILDREN TO SLEEP

While on a trip you might not always get a crib at your destination, and carrying one will make life all the more difficult. Instead call ahead to see if there are any cribs or roll out beds for children. You may even put blankets on the floor. Weave them a story about camping and they will gladly sleep without any trouble.

32. GET BABY PRODUCTS DELIVERED AT YOUR DESTINATION

If you are absolutely paranoid about not getting your favourite variety of diaper or brand of baby food, check out online stores like amazon.com for services in your destination city. You can buy things online ahead of your travel and get them delivered to your hotel upon arrival.

33. FEEDING NEEDS OF YOUR INFANTS

If you are travelling with a breastfed infant, you save the trouble of carrying bottles and bottle sanitization kits. For special food, or medications, you may need to call ahead to make sure you have a refrigerator where you are staying.

34. FEEDING NEEDS OF YOUR TODDLER

With the progression from infancy to toddler, their dietary requirements too evolve. You will have to pack some snacks for travelling time. Fresh fruits and vegetables can be purchased at your destination. Most of the cities you travel to in whichever part of the world, will have baby food products and formulas, available at the local drug-store or the supermarket.

35. PICKING CLOTHES FOR YOUR BABY

Contrary to popular belief, babies can do without many changes of clothes. At the most pack 2 outfits per day. Pack mix and match type clothes for your little one as well. Pick things which are comfortable to wear and quick to dry.

36. SELECTING SHOES FOR YOUR BABY

Like outfits, kids can make do with two pairs of comfortable shoes. If you can get some water resistant shoes it will be best. To expedite drying wet shoes, you can stuff newspaper in them then wrap them with newspaper and leave them to dry overnight.

37. KEEP ONE CHANGE OF CLOTHES HANDY

Travelling with kids can be tricky. Keep a change of clothes for the kids and mum handy in your purse or tote bag. This takes a bit of space in your hand luggage but comes extremely handy in case there are any accidents or spills.

38. LEAVE BEHIND BABY ACCESSORIES

Baby accessories like their bed, bath tub, car seat, crib etc. should be left at home. Many hotels provide a crib on request, while car seats can be borrowed from friends or rented. Babies can be given a bath in the hotel sink or even in the adult bath tub with a little bit of water. If you bring a few bath toys, they can be used in the bath, pool, and out of water. They can also be sanitized easily in the sink.

39. CARRY A SMALL LOAD OF PLASTIC BAGS

With children around there are chances of a number of soiled clothes and diapers. These plastic bags help to sort the dirt from the clean inside your big bag.

These are very light weight and come in handy to other carry stuff as well at times.

PACK WITH A PURPOSE

40. PACKING FOR BUSINESS TRIPS

One neutral-colored suit should suffice. It can be paired with different shirts, ties and accessories for different occasions. One pair of black suit pants could be worn with a matching jacket for the office or with a snazzy top for dinner.

41. PACKING FOR A CRUISE

Most cruises have formal dinners, and that formal dress usually takes up a lot of space. However you might find a tuxedo to rent. For women, a short black dress with multiple accessory options will do the trick.

42. PACKING FOR A LONG TRIP OVER DIFFERENT CLIMATES

The secret packing mantra for travel over multiple climates is layering. Layering traps air around your body creating insulation against the cold. The same light t-shirt that is comfortable in a warmer climate can be the innermost layer in a colder climate.

REDUCE SOME MORE WEIGHT

43. LEAVE PRECIOUS THINGS AT HOME

Things that you would hate to lose or get damaged leave them at home. Precious jewelry, expensive gadgets or dresses, could be anything. You will not require these on your trip. Leave them at home and spare the load on your mind.

44. SEND SOUVENIRS BY MAIL

If you have spent all your money on purchasing souvenirs, carrying them back in the same bag that you brought along would be difficult. Either pack everything in another bag and check it in the airport or get everything shipped to your home. Use an international carrier for a secure transit, but this could be more expensive than the checking fees at the airport.

45. AVOID CARRYING BOOKS

Books equal to weight. There are many reading apps which you can download on your smart phone or tab.

Plus there are gadgets like Kindle and Nook that are thinner and lighter alternatives to your regular book.

CHECK, GET, SET, CHECK AGAIN

46. STRATEGIZE BEFORE PACKING

Create a travel list and prepare all that you think you need to carry along. Keep everything on your bed or floor before packing and then think through once again – do I really need that? Any item that meets this question can be avoided. Remove whatever you don't really need and pack the rest.

47. TEST YOUR LUGGAGE

Once you have fully packed for the trip take a test trip with your luggage. Take your bags and go to town for window shopping for an hour. If you enjoy your hour long trip it is good to go, if not, go home and reduce the load some more. Repeat this test till you hit the right weight.

48. ADD A ROLL OF DUCT TAPE

You might wonder why, when this book has been talking about reducing stuff, we're suddenly asking you to pack something totally unusual. This is because when you have limited supplies, duct tape is immensely helpful for small repairs – a broken bag, leaking zip-lock bag, broken sunglasses, you name it and duct tape can fix it, temporarily.

49. LIST OF ESSENTIAL ITEMS

Even though the emphasis is on packing light, there are things which have to be carried for any trip. Here is our list of essentials:

•Passport/Visa or any other ID

•Any other paper work that might be required on a trip like permits, hotel reservation confirmations etc.

•Medicines – all your prescription medicines and emergency kit, especially if you are travelling with children

•Medical or vaccination records

•Money in foreign currency if travelling to a different country

•Tickets- Email or Message them to your phone

50. MAKE THE MOST OF YOUR TRIP

Wherever you are going, whatever you hope to do we encourage you to embrace it whole-heartedly. Take in the scenery, the culture and above all, enjoy your time away from home.

On a long journey even a straw weighs heavy.

-Spanish Proverb

PACKING AND PLANNING TIPS

A Week before Leaving

- Arrange for someone to take care of pets and water plants.

- Stop mail and newspaper.

- Notify Credit Card companies where you are going.

- Change your thermostat settings.

- Car inspected, oil is changed, and tires have the correct pressure.

- Passports and photo identification is up to date.

- Pay bills.

- Copy important items and download travel Apps.

- Start collecting small bills for tips.

Right Before Leaving

- Clean out refrigerator.

- Empty garbage cans.

- Lock windows.

- Make sure you have the proper identification with you.

- Bring cash for tips.

- Remember travel documents.

- Lock door behind you.

- Remember wallet.

- Unplug items in house and pack chargers.

>TOURIST

READ OTHER
GREATER THAN A TOURIST
BOOKS

>TOURIST

> TOURIST

Visit Greater Than a Tourist for Free Travel Tips
http://GreaterThanATourist.com

Sign up for the Greater Than a Tourist Newsletter for
discount days, new books, and travel information:
http://eepurl.com/cxspyf

Follow us on Facebook for tips, images, and ideas:
https://www.facebook.com/GreaterThanATourist

Follow us on Pinterest for travel tips and ideas:
http://pinterest.com/GreaterThanATourist

Follow us on Instagram for beautiful travel images:
http://Instagram.com/GreaterThanATourist

>TOURIST

> TOURIST

Please leave your honest review of this book on Amazon and Goodreads. Please send your feedback to GreaterThanaTourist@gmail.com as we continue to improve the series. We appreciate your positive and constructive feedback. Thank you.

METRIC CONVERSIONS

TEMPERATURE

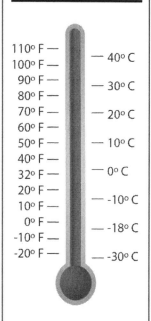

110° F —   — 40° C
100° F —
90° F —   — 30° C
80° F —
70° F —   — 20° C
60° F —
50° F —   — 10° C
40° F —
32° F —   — 0° C
20° F —
10° F —   — -10° C
0° F —
-10° F —   — -18° C
-20° F —   — -30° C

To convert F to C:

Subtract 32, and then multiply by 5/9 or .5555.

To Convert C to F:

Multiply by 1.8 and then add 32.

32F = 0C

LIQUID VOLUME

To Convert:.................Multiply by
U.S. Gallons to Liters................ 3.8
U.S. Liters to Gallons 26
Imperial Gallons to U.S. Gallons 1.2
Imperial Gallons to Liters....... 4.55
Liters to Imperial Gallons 22
1 Liter = .26 U.S. Gallon
1 U.S. Gallon = 3.8 Liters

DISTANCE

To convert ....Multiply by
Inches to Centimeters 2.54
Centimeters to Inches 39
Feet to Meters...................... .3
Meters to Feet 3.28
Yards to Meters 91
Meters to Yards 1.09
Miles to Kilometers 1.61
Kilometers to Miles............ .62
1 Mile = 1.6 km
1 km = .62 Miles

WEIGHT

1 Ounce = .28 Grams
1 Pound = .4555 Kilograms
1 Gram = .04 Ounce
1 Kilogram = 2.2 Pounds

TRAVEL QUESTIONS

- Do you bring presents home to family or friends after a vacation?

- Do you get motion sick?

- Do you have a favorite billboard?

- Do you know what to do if there is a flat tire?

- Do you like a sun roof open?

- Do you like to eat in the car?

- Do you like to wear sun glasses in the car?

- Do you like toppings on your ice cream?

- Do you use public bathrooms?

- Did you bring your cell phone and does it have power?

- Do you have a form of identification with you?

- Have you ever been pulled over by a cop?

- Have you ever given money to a stranger on a road trip?

- Have you ever taken a road trip with animals?

- Have you ever went on a vacation alone?

- Have you ever run out of gas?

- If you could move to any place in the world, where would it be?

- If you could travel anywhere in the world, where would you travel?

- If you could travel in any vehicle, which one would it be?

- If you had three things to wish for from a magic genie, what would they be?

- If you have a driver's license, how many times did it take you to pass the test?

- What are you the most afraid of on vacation?

- What do you want to get away from the most when you are on vacation?

- What foods smells bad to you?

- What item do you bring on ever trip with you away from home?

- What makes you sleepy?

- What song would you love to hear on the radio when you're cruising on the highway?

- What travel job would you want the least?

- What will you miss most while you are away from home?

- What is something you always wanted to try?

- What is the best road side attraction that you ever saw?

- What is the farthest distance you ever biked?

- What is the farthest distance you ever walked?

- What is the weirdest thing you needed to buy while on vacation?

- What is your favorite candy?

- What is your favorite color car?

- What is your favorite family vacation?

- What is your favorite food?

- What is your favorite gas station drink or food?

- What is your favorite license plate design?

- What is your favorite restaurant?

- What is your favorite smell?

- What is your favorite song?

- What is your favorite sound that nature makes?

- What is your favorite thing to bring home from a vacation?

- What is your favorite vacation with friends?

- What is your favorite way to relax?

- Where is the farthest place you ever traveled in a car?

- Where is the farthest place you ever went North, South, East and West?

- Where is your favorite place in the world?

- Who is your favorite singer?

- Who taught you how to drive?

- Who will you miss the most while you are away?

- Who if the first person you will contact when you get to your destination?

- Who brought you on your first vacation?

- Who likes to travel the most in your life?

- Would you rather be hot or cold?

- Would you rather drive above, below, or at the speed limited?

- Would you rather drive on a highway or a back road?

- Would you rather go on a train or a boat?

- Would you rather go to the beach or the woods?

TRAVEL BUCKET LIST

1.

2.

3.

4.

5.

6.

7.

8.

9.

10.